A thesaurus is a book full of very useful words.

USBORNE
Big Picture
THESAURUS

Written by
Rosie Hore

Illustrated by
Rachael Saunders

Designed by
Emily Barden

In this book, you'll find lists of words with similar meanings to help you find new words to use.

You'll also find opposites...

...and ways of describing things precisely. Instead of walk, try...

daring, bold, courageous

bad
evil

good
kind

tiptoe, sneak, creep

Contents

TWEET

See how many times you can spot us in this book.

yellow
lemon — gold

red
crimson scarle
ruby tomat

wash
clean
scrub

WHIZ — journey, trip, outing

HIKING TRAIL

CAMPGROUND

BAA

MMM

yummy
tasty
delicious

tall
high
towering

hike, trek, walk

swell, churn, froth

leafy
lush

windy
gusty
breezy

sandy, dusty, dry

SNORT

Keep on going!

Home and family

Where do you live?

house
cottage
condo
apartment
mobile home
houseboat
mansion

Homes can be...

big
grand
lavish

or...

small
cozy
comfortable
snug

Houses can have...

a roof
an upstairs
a downstairs
floors
windows
a basement
a front door
a back door
a yard
a patio

Playroom

toys
games
activities

cuddle
hug
embrace

HMM

GIGGLE

Bedroom

asleep
dozing

wake up
get up

DRING
DRING

untidy
messy
chaotic

Bathroom
restroom
toilet

Kitchen

mop, wipe

slip
trip

clean
straighten
put away

Living room

cook
prepare
make

nap
snoo

drapes
curtains

throw away
get rid of
discard
chuck out
toss

Why is it
always me w
takes out th
trash?

meeow

Good morning!
You've got letters,
packages and a
present today.

sweep, brush

RUFF

Getting around

You can
go on a...
journey
trip
outing
excursion
ride
voyage
tour

car

What a nice day for a drive.

Buy your tickets on board.

bus

Planes... fly, take off
WHOOSH
airplane

Journeys can be...
short *or* long
quick *or* slow
bumpy *or* smooth
one-way *or* round-trip
on time *or* delayed
planned *or* surprise

baggage
cases
luggage

overtake, pass

motorcycle

speed up
accelerate

delivery bike
moped

Cars have...
wheels
tires
an engine
a windshield
seat belts
a hood
headlights
front seats
back seats
a steering wheel
a trunk
bumpers
brakes

BANG!
crash
accident
collision
smash
BOOM!

GAS STATION

Pay here!

gas, fuel, gasoline, diesel

RELIABLE MOVERS

Trucks...
carry
transport
deliver

hiss

Not so fast!

broken down

Boats might...
float, drift,
cruise, steam

splash

paddle boat

rowboat

VAROOM

speedboat

Colors, shapes and patterns

blue

cobalt

sky blue   sapphire   aqua

striped   lined

Navy is a dark shade of blue.

turquoise

Where's the dog with the blue leash?

yellow

lemon

sunny   saffron

spotted   dotted   polka dot

mustard

ocher   gold

Where's the multicolored candy store?

red

tomato   cherry

ruby   scarlet

zigzag

green

bottle green   apple green   grass green

lime   olive   khaki

plaid   checkered   gingham

jade

emerald

pink

coral   cerise

salmon   magenta   fuchsia

brown

fawn   buff   hazel

wavy   wiggly   squiggly

beige   bronze

Measuring and investigating

What size?

huge, gigantic, enormous

big
large

small
little
mini

tiny
minute
miniscule

width

wider
broader

narrower
thinner

height

taller

shorter

length

longer

shorter

getting bigger
growing
expanding
enlarging
swelling

getting smaller
shrinking
decreasing
reducing
dwindling

PUFF

How heavy?

balanced, equal, same

unbalanced

heavy
weighty

light
lightweight

BOB

float

sink

How far?

distance, extent, range

near
close
nearby

far
distant
far away

How many?

count 1 2 3 4 5 6 7 8 9 10

add
plus
tally
total

amount
quantity
number

several
many
lots
loads

few
hardly any
not many
a couple

adding

subtracting
taking away

double

half

dividing
sharing
splitting

whole
complete

piece
part
fraction
segment
section

What is it made of?

plastic

rubber

metal

stone

glass

wood

paper

cloth

clay

What does it feel like?

hard *or* soft
rough *or* smooth
sharp *or* rounded
stiff *or* stretchy
firm *or* squishy

fluffy

Comparisons

shallow

deep

deeper

empty

full
filled

overflowing

matching
identical

similar
alike

different
clashing

Your body

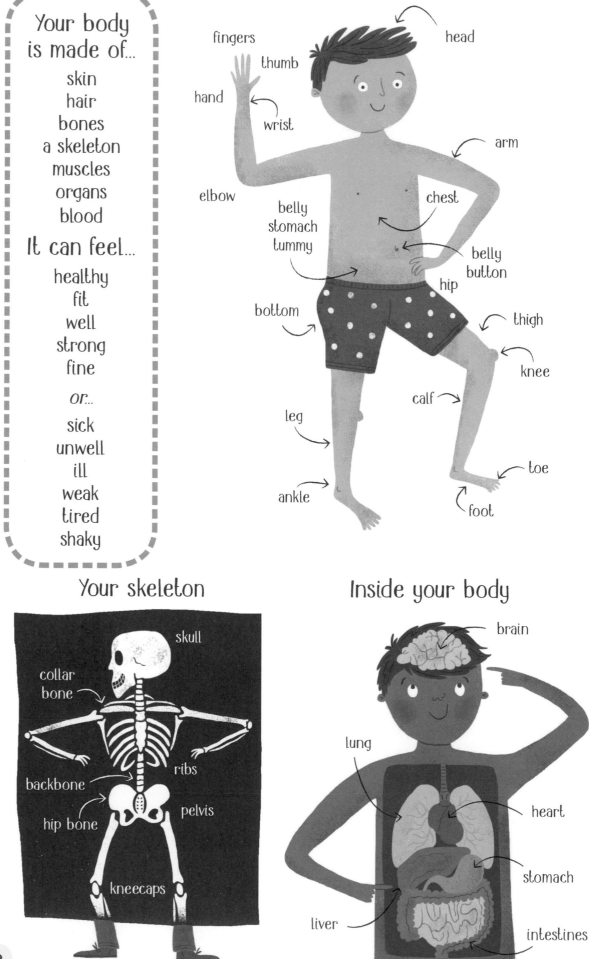

Your body
is made of...
skin
hair
bones
a skeleton
muscles
organs
blood

It can feel...
healthy
fit
well
strong
fine

or...
sick
unwell
ill
weak
tired
shaky

fingers
thumb
hand
wrist
elbow
head
arm
chest
belly
stomach
tummy
belly
button
hip
bottom
thigh
knee
calf
leg
toe
ankle
foot

Your skeleton

skull
collar
bone
backbone
hip bone
ribs
pelvis
kneecaps

Inside your body

brain
lung
heart
stomach
liver
intestines

Parts of your face
forehead
eyebrows
eyes
eyelids
eyelashes
ears
nose
nostrils
mouth
lips
teeth
tongue
chin
neck
cheeks

Your senses

seeing

smelling

hearing

tasting

touching

12

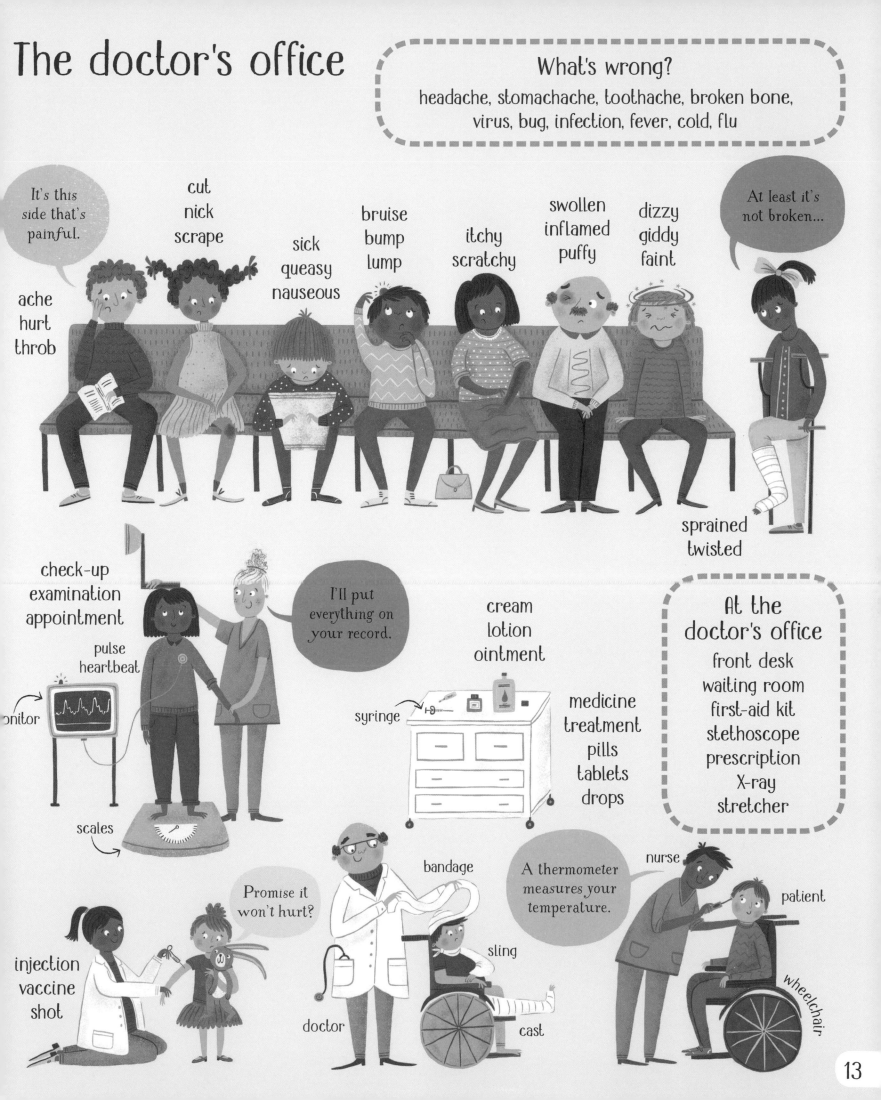

Describing people

People can look...
- pretty
- beautiful
- handsome
- attractive
- glamorous
- fashionable
- stylish
- cool
- neat
- shabby
- scruffy
- unusual
- unique
- individual

tall
lanky

short
little
petite

husky
stout
stocky

thin
skinny
slim

Ha ha, I look so gangly!

freckles

SPIN SPIN

twiddle

I remember being in the circus!

bald

baby
toddler

child
kid

teenager
young person

adult
grown-up

old
elderly

Hair can be...
- long
- short
- curly
- frizzy
- straight
- wavy
- wiry
- tangled
- glossy

Hair colors

blonde
fair

black
dark

brown
brunette

red
auburn

gray
silvery

People can be...

helpful, nice, kind, thoughtful, funny, witty, friendly, honest, talented,
unkind, nosy, boring, annoying, selfish, lazy, mean, rude, greedy

chatty
talkative

or...

quiet
silent

reckless
rash

or...

sensible
practical

That looks far too dangerous.

silly
bizarre
odd
wacky
peculiar
quirky

or...

serious
stern
solemn

strong
muscular
beefy

or...

weak
puny
feeble

GASP

graceful
elegant
poised

or...

clumsy
accident-prone
awkward

Whoops!

SPLAT

polite
well mannered
well behaved

or...

cheeky
mischievous
naughty

curtsey

15

How are you feeling?

I'm feeling HAPPY!

happy
in a good mood
glad
joyful

whistle

cheerful
jolly
upbeat

When you're
happy you...
smile
grin
beam
laugh
giggle
chuckle

Best day
ever!

delighted
ecstatic

I'm feeling SAD.

sad
unhappy
low
gloomy
miserable

When you're
unhappy you...
frown
cry
sob
whine
sulk

moody
grumpy
snippy

hurt
upset

devastated

I'm feeling SCARED.

scared
frightened
afraid

nibble

anxious
nervous
worried

terrified
petrified
fearful

When you're
scared you...
scream
shriek
jump
shake
shiver

I'm feeling ANGRY.

angry
grumpy
moody
upset

ARRRRRR

furious
livid

When you're
angry you...
scowl
shout
huff
yell
argue

You don't
understand!

annoyed
frustrated

16

Liking and disliking

like
enjoy

love
adore

dislike

hate
loathe
detest

unsure
cautious
wary

I'm not sure about this...

This is going to be fun!

excited
enthusiastic

wobble

It's not as high as I wanted...

disappointed

WHEEE!

thrilled
exhilarated

I did it!

proud
pleased

There's nothing to do.

HUMPH

How come she gets the best stuff?

bored   calm   smug   envious

I'm looking for the parking lot.

scratch

blush

I'm so sorry.

shocked
surprised

Come and play!

confused
puzzled
bewildered

embarrassed

shy
timid

confident
bold

BLEURGH

Animals

Animals can have...

a tail
paws
claws
spines
horns
fangs
hooves
whiskers
antlers
quills
a trunk

GRRR
ROAR

wild
fierce
ferocious

rare
uncommon
endangered

crunch

Awesome! I've never seen a panda in real life before.

PAT
tame
obedient
WAG

Animals that only eat plants are known as herbivores.

sleepy
dozy
drowsy

alert
attentive
watchful
wary

camouflaged
disguised
hidden

Animals that only eat meat are known as carnivores.

A bear's fur is...
soft
fuzzy
bushy
shaggy

lap

A panther's coat is...
shiny
silky
sleek
lick

A crocodile's skin is...
scaly, dry, rough, bumpy

Foods and drinks

Food can be...
- raw
- cooked
- broiled
- fried
- baked
- boiled
- charred
- steamed
- barbecued
- roasted

Ingredients can be...
- sliced
- chopped
- mashed
- puréed

yummy
tasty
delicious

disgusting
revolting
nasty

GULP

sour
sharp
tart
tangy

MMMM

sweet
sugary
syrupy

munch

salty
savory
seasoned

smelly
stinky
strong

WHIFF

dry
stale

crumble

SPLASH

juicy
fresh
ripe

Vegetables

cucumber

melon

lemon

potato

broccoli

lettuce

onion

eggplants

chilies

carrot

cabbage

dat

Fish

tuna

mussels

salmon

lobster

shrimp

cod

steak

Meat

sausage

beef

bacon

lamb

chicken

In the refrigerator

butter

cream

milk

cheese

eggs

yogurt

20

Fruit

grapes
apple
berries
orange
tomato
pomegranate
bananas

In the pantry

rice
cereal
couscous
bread
noodles
pasta
beans
nuts
spices
herbs
pastries
salt
pepper
oil
flour
chocolate
sugar
honey

Drinks

water
tea
coffee
juice
soda

bubbly
sparkling

SLURP

mild
bland
tasteless

spicy
peppery
hot

CHOMP

crispy
crunchy

oily
greasy

creamy
gooey
gloopy
sticky

Eating

You might be...
hungry
starving
ravenous
famished

or...
full
stuffed
satisfied

What do you eat with?
knife
fork
spoon
chopsticks
your fingers

carton

bowl

plate

How do you eat?
nibble
bite
chew

or...

scarf
devour
munch
guzzle

Meals
breakfast
lunch
snack
dinner
supper
feast

dessert

In a city

Cities can be...
busy
crowded
lively
hectic
buzzing
bustling
famous
expensive
diverse
sprawling

You can walk down...
roads
paths
sidewalks
alleys
avenues
streets
lanes
passages
boulevards
backstreets

Places with food
restaurant
coffee shop
takeout
café
supermarket

ice cream vendor

zipline

slide

playground

swimming pool

fountain

skyscraper

library

park bench

SCHOOL

statue

DING DING

DONG

$

BANK

train station

I'm late for work – again!

art gallery

THEATER

canal

Will we see the mosque from the canal?

HOSPITAL

ambulance

SUPERMARKET

police station

AIRPORT

terminal

parking lot

aircraft   ZOOOOM

runway

Buildings can be...
new
modern
contemporary

church

BING BONG

tower block

STADIUM

fans

CHEER

Everything half price! Only today!

market stall

business
company
firm

office

Movie theater
3D Mega Screens

fire station

post office   hair salon   bakery   butcher shop

minaret

subway
metro

Hindu temple

Which way is the park?

mall

mosque

MUSEUM

shoppers

synagogue

BEEP

Buildings can be made of...

glass
concrete
bricks
stone
metal
wood

Places in the city
city center
district
area
neighborhood
block
suburb
outskirts
main street
shopping district
business district

demolish
knock down
bulldoze

crane

I'm building the new City Hall.

build
construct
put up

building site

old
traditional
historic

ancient
in ruins
ruined

derelict
ramshackle
rundown

In the countryside

The countryside can be...
peaceful
quiet
tranquil
serene
scenic
rural
rustic

The scenery is...
beautiful
breathtaking
awe-inspiring
glorious
picturesque
impressive

Paths can be...
crooked
winding
twisting
curving
bumpy
uphill *or* downhill
grassy *or* bare
steep *or* flat

summit
top
peak

mountain

woods
forest

Lots to do on the farm today.

tractor

hay bales

field
meadow
pasture

wildflowers

hedgerow

woof

sheep dog

farmer

gate

close
shut

fence

path, lane, track

Streams...
gurgle
babble
bubble
tinkle
trickle

Waterfalls...
gush
cascade
surge

hike
wander
ramble

How many fish can you see?

Rivers...
flow
stream
rush

riverbank

muddy
boggy
marshy

explore
investigate
discover

boulder

stone

pebbles

rock

24

Trees and flowers

Trees can have...
a trunk
branches
twigs
leaves
bark
roots
fruit
nuts
sap

They can be...
dense
leafy
green
lush
or...
sparse
bare
thin
bald

Trunks are...
strong
hardy
mighty

rabbit

sniff

Branches can be...
bent, twisted, gnarled
or...
straight, smooth, solid

Vines...
wind, twine, coil

Bark can be...
tough
rough
knobbly

Seedlings...
grow
sprout
shoot up
develop
take root

CHEEP CHIRP

bird's nest

squirrel

acorns

hole
hollow

Twigs are...
brittle
dry
They...
splinter
break

Leaves...
fall
drop
tumble

Some trees have
needles
spines
thorns
cones

mushroom
toadstool
fungus

worms

ear

Flowers...
blossom
bloom

petal

leaf

blade
of grass

caterpillar

MUNCH

brrrr

Flowers
have...
a stem
petals
seeds
buds

They are...
pretty
bright
colorful
vibrant
sweet-smelling
fragrant

butterfly

FLAP

FLAP

bumblebee

Seeds...
spread
disperse
scatter

wilt
wither
shrivel

seed
head

Stems...
support
hold up
carry

stamen

pollen

droop, bend, bow, nod

Thistles
are...
prickly
spiky
sharp

Seed pods...
pop
burst
crack

shoot

bulb

bud

soil
earth
mud

The undergrowth is...
wild, tangled, overgrown

The weather

Wet weather is...
rainy
drizzly
cloudy
cool
refreshing

rainbow

raincloud

sunshine
beams
rays

Sunny weather is...
hot
warm
fine
pleasant
balmy

The sky is...
blue
clear
cloudless

drizzle   deluge   shower   downpour   rainstorm   cloudburst

I'm fed up with this rain.

What games shall we play?

drenched
soaking
dripping wet

soggy
damp

YOWL

puddle

bare feet

basket

picnic food

BZZZZ

hood

umbrella

cap   sunglasses   sunhat

You'll need a...
coat
raincoat
parka
sweater
jacket
and...
rain boots
rubber boots

Put on some sunscreen – it's blazing.

shorts

sandals

SPLASH

28

Where on Earth?

horizon

sand dunes

camel

Only a few hours to the next camp.

TRUDGE

expedition, journey, trek

palm trees

An oasis is...
cool, fresh, refreshing

desert foxes

lap

scorpion

SCUTTLE

The land is...

dry   baked
sandy   bare
dusty   barren
scorched   parched

The desert heat is...
blistering
sweltering
searing
fiery

cactus

In the
jungle, it's...
wet
damp
steamy
humid
muggy
sticky

Jungle animals...
buzz
screech
growl
hum
shriek
squawk

PACAW!

hiss

spider's web

DRIP

DRIP

vine

Sap...
dribbles
trickles
oozes

Jaguars...
prowl
stalk
hunt

Venus flytrap

SNAP

The forest floor is...
dark, gloomy, shady, shadowy

Playing sports

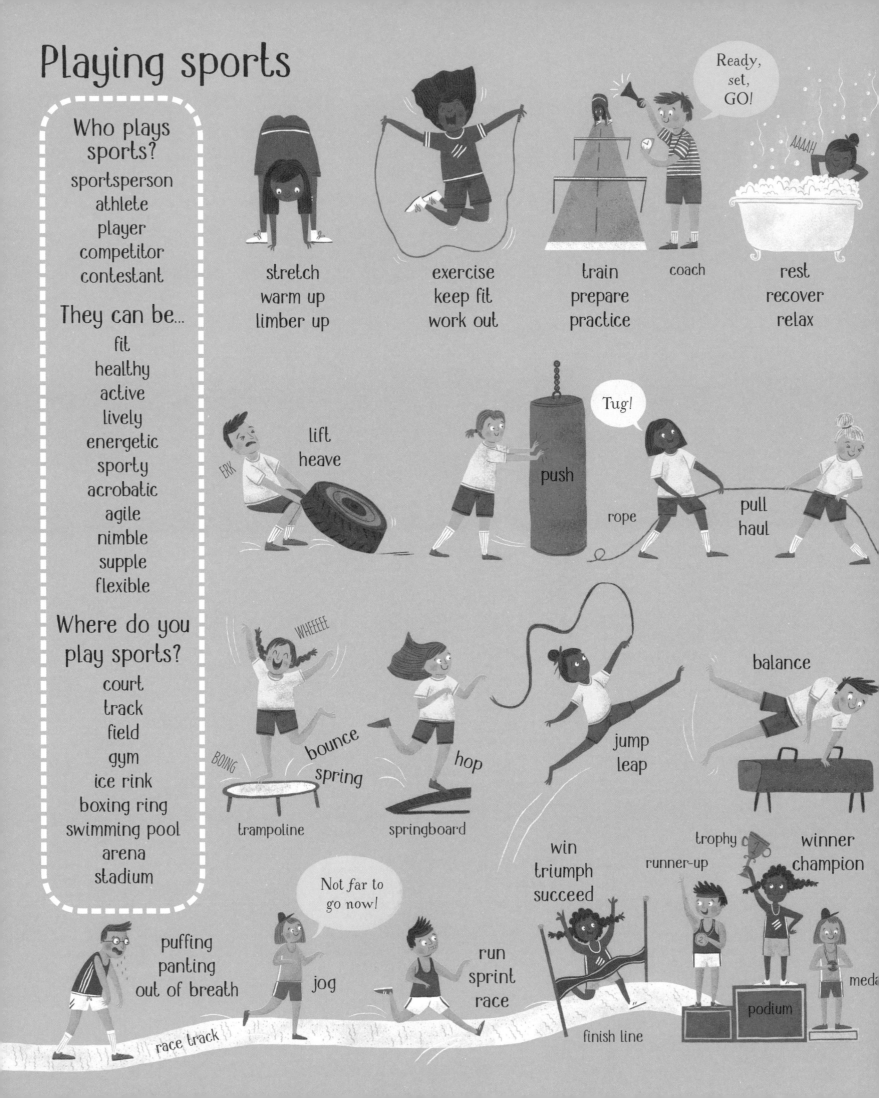

Who plays
sports?
sportsperson
athlete
player
competitor
contestant

They can be...
fit
healthy
active
lively
energetic
sporty
acrobatic
agile
nimble
supple
flexible

Where do you
play sports?
court
track
field
gym
ice rink
boxing ring
swimming pool
arena
stadium

stretch
warm up
limber up

exercise
keep fit
work out

train
prepare
practice

coach

Ready, set, GO!

AAAAH

rest
recover
relax

ERK

lift
heave

Tug!

push

rope

pull
haul

WHEEEEE

BOING

bounce
spring

trampoline

hop

springboard

jump
leap

balance

win
triumph
succeed

trophy
runner-up

winner
champion

Not far to go now!

puffing
panting
out of breath

jog

run
sprint
race

podium

medal

race track

finish line

What do you need?
equipment
gear

racket
ball

tennis racket

boxing gloves

baseball
glove

badminton
racket

shuttlecock

ballet
shoes

basketball

table tennis
paddle

ice hockey stick
and puck

tennis ball

cricket bat

leg
pads

goggles

knee
pads

weights

bicycle
helmet

football

skis

roller
skates

climbing ropes

yoga mat

WHOOOOOOOOSH

throw
lob
fling

catch
grab
grasp
clutch

THWACK

hit
whack
smash

TOWN TIGERS

CITY CUBS

scoreboard

DOH!

miss

supporters
fans
followers

WHOOP!

Teams enter a...
tournament
match
game
competition
contest

applaud
cheer

SCORE

GOAAAAAL!

shoot

goalkeeper

dive
lunge

They are...
competitive
determined
focused

kick, pass

They might...
win
draw
lose

dodge
weave

cheat
foul

Hey!
Play fairly.

dribble

tackle

referee

33

Telling a story

Choose an option from each box to tell a story.

WHEN?

Long, long ago...

Last Tuesday...

Once upon a time...

When I was a baby...

On an ordinary morning...

In the middle of the night...

At the beginning of time...

palace

castle

In Outer Space...

space station

otherworldly
unearthly

secret den

under the bed

WHERE?

desert island

faraway
distant
exotic
far-flung

school

familiar
everyday
normal
ordinary

A deep, dark forest...

magical
enchanted
fairytale

CLANK

WHIR

robot

vampire

mermaid

WHO?

princess

Fe, fi, fo, fum.

ARGH

giant

Grandma

I can fly!

unexpected
abnormal
out-of-the-ordinary

adventure
quest
mission

WHAT HAPPENS?

first of all
suddenly
instantly
all at once

ZAP

spell
enchantment
curse

splish

dab

invention
breakthrough
discovery

WHO DO THEY MEET?

werewolf

magician

astronaut

spy

dragon

genie

WHAT WILL THEY NEED?

getaway car

secret identity

clue

disguise

sidekick

spaceship

WHAT HAPPENS NEXT?
then
afterward
finally

problem
glitch
mishap

mix-up
confusion

surprise
shock
bombshell

plot
plan
heist

WHAT HAPPENS IN THE END?
cliffhanger
homecoming
reunion
mystery solved

escape
getaway

happily ever after

tragedy
sad ending

party
celebration
happy ending

Explorers are...
adventurous
intrepid
fearless

Inventors are...
intelligent
clever
brainy

X-ray goggles

Prepare to be saved, world!

Superheroes are...
mighty
powerful
invincible

Warriors are...
gifted
skilled
talented

SWIPE

Heroes...

Heroes can be...
brave
bold
courageous
plucky
kind
generous
good-hearted
magical
extraordinary
exceptional
remarkable
amazing
astounding

sword   armor

Sir Steve to the rescue!

shield

Knights are...
valiant
chivalrous
gallant

They...
fight
battle
combat

Princes and princesses are...
royal, regal, noble

wave

carriage

footman

Ways of speaking

say
tell
ask
answer
exclaim
mumble
whimper
snarl
babble
beg
sneer

boast
brag
gloat

moan
sigh
groan

cackle
croak
crow

shout
yell
bellow

whisper
murmur
mutter

BRAAAINS

Zombies are...
cursed
jinxed
doomed

Aliens...
attack, invade, strike

Take me to your leader.

WOOOOOOOOOOOO

Ghosts are...
spooky, ghoulish, eerie, paranormal

They...
haunt
torment
plague

Villains can be...
evil
wicked
nasty
cowardly
spineless
awful
fierce
vicious
grotesque
horrible
ghastly
gruesome

RIP

...and villains

Pirates are...
notorious
wanted
infamous

eye patch

They...
steal
loot
thieve

treasure

wooden leg

Lock him in the dungeon!

crown

Evil queens are...
ruthless
savage
brutal

GRRR

Monsters are...
frightening, terrifying, menacing

Ways of moving

march
stride
stroll
totter
lumber
lurch
saunter
trudge
stumble
shuffle
crawl

tiptoe
creep
sneak

stomp, tramp, stamp

swagger
parade
strut

limp
hobble
stagger

Puzzles and games

Find the opposites

Can you match each word to its opposite?

old

sour

pastel

tame

sweet

delighted

devastated

young

wild

bright

Missing words

One word in each sentence is missing.
Can you pick the best word to fill the gap?

1. I'm the .... monster in the land.

fiercest
cutest
cleanest

2. This chili is too ....!

spicy
scary
sporty

3. Yippee, we .... the game.

lost
won
threw

4. We love .... in the countryside.

driving
hiking
scrubbing

5. I've hurt my ....

shoulder
hand
leg

6. Hey! Stop being so ....

shy
greedy
friendly

7. My hair is ....

curly
chatty
salty

8. We're all in the ....

car
boat
plane

Word match

Which word in the list below could you use instead?

angry
hungry
furious
glad

enormous
careful
narrow
huge

creep
sneak
sprint
shout

sporty
athletic
lazy
sparkly

sleepy
cool
gray
dozy

Mixed-up stories

These two stories have been mixed up. Can you put them in the right order?

Spotting game

Look back through the book to find the answers to these questions.

Spotting game
1. page 25
2. page 29
3. pages 25 and 28
4. pages 6 and 24
5. page 22
6. page 20
7. four times: on pages 2, 7, 9 and 22

Mixed-up stories
A, D, B, C.
1, 4, 3, 2.

Word match
sleepy - dozy
sporty - athletic
creep - sneak
enormous - huge
angry - furious

Missing words
1. fiercest
2. spicy
3. won
4. hiking
5. leg
6. greedy
7. curly
8. car

Find the opposites
old - young
pastel - bright
sweet - sour
devastated - delighted
wild - tame

USBORNE QUICKLINKS

For links to websites with word games and activities, go to the Usborne Quicklinks website at **www.usborne.com/quicklinks** and type in the title of this book.

We recommend that children are supervised while on the internet.

MANAGING EDITOR: Ruth Brocklehurst   MANAGING DESIGNER: Nickey Butler   LITERACY CONSULTANT: Kerenza Ghosh

First published in 2017 by Usborne Publishing Ltd., 83-85 Saffron Hill, London, EC1N 8RT. England. www.usborne.com Copyright © 2017 Usborne Publishing Ltd.